Thanks for
animal Support.
Much Love
Tom + Charli-Me Cos
6/20/23

This book is dedicated to my loving and supportive husband, Dr. Thomas Schopler who gave me the confidence and support to get this book published.

A Beautiful Story About
Charli the Cat

THERESA ELIZABETH SCHOPLER

ISBN: 978-1-66787-560-6

Adopting an animal like Charli to give
them a forever loving home.

Mr. Joey was not looking to adopt a cat.

An ad with a beautiful photo of a black and white tuxedo cat named Charli caught his attention.

Mr. Joey decided to check out the ad.

PLEASE HELP!! URGENT!!! One of my friends took in this sweet female cat from a neighbor that passed away but unfortunately she does not get along with her older cat and she will have to take her to a shelter if she does not find someone to adopt her. Charli is a sweet, cuddly and playful 2 year old female. She would need to go to a home with either no cats or with young ones. I am committed to help her find Charli a good home, not take her to a shelter. Please let me know if anyone is interested in adopting Charli. Thank you.

He saw Charli and picked her up with no second thoughts.

She snuggled with him. Mr. Joey decided to adopt Charli and take her home with him. Thus, giving her a loving forever home with her Forever Dad.

After Mr. Joey took Charli home and put her down on the floor, he could not find her. Strangely, he questioned if somehow Charli had gotten outside. Mr. Joey searched everywhere. Eventually, after an exhausting search, he heard a faint bell sound that came from the necklace around her neck. He found her hiding in the tv cabinet. Lovingly, Mr. Joey reached up and pulled her out. He gave her some food. From then on, it was a magical love between Mr. Joey and Charli, the cat.

Charli adjusted well to her forever home
and Mr. Joey became her Forever Dad.

Charli loves to sleep in the Chewy box.

Charli loves to squeeze in boxes.

Sylvester, the cat is Charli's favorite
stuffed animal to cuddle with.

Charli looks out everyday and is content.

Charli watching the rain fall. Charli is fascinated
and meets the new baby bird Samantha.

Charli likes to balance and pose.

Charli pats down the bed before
she settles in for the night.

Now everyday in her new home, Charli would look outside and she became friends with the outside creatures. For you see, Charli has already made many friends, such as beautiful swans, birds, ducks, turtles, iguanas, lizards, and peacocks. Charli watches them play.

Olive Oyl, the Peacock and Harley,
the Cat waiting for Charli to come outside.

Charli looks to go outside to be with her friends.

One day, her Forever Dad, Mr. Joey let her go outside to meet and play with her outside friends.

Charli peeks in her home when
she is ready to come in.

Charli always returns to her forever home.

Charli peeks outside to watch Harley
do tricks for her attention.

Harley, Charli's cat friend.

Charli looks out as Harley playfully sits
on the canvas roof to watch her.

When her Forever Dad, Mr. Joey got sick, Charli
would faithfully stay by his side to offer him comfort,
companionship, and much love with snuggles.

Charli playing around.

Charli waits patiently for someone to
come home and play with her.

Now Charli was still very shy around people.

Mr. Joey brought Charli to meet Ms. Theresa for the first time. They instantly fell in love with each other and Ms. Theresa became her Forever Mom.

For you see, Ms. Theresa never had any real contact with animals in her life. When Ms. Theresa saw Charli, she reached down and picked Charli up. Charli, although still shy around people, cuddled with Ms. Theresa and they immediately played together.

Charli loves to cuddle with her Mom at bedtime.

Charli loves to play and pose with her
Forever Mom, Ms. Theresa.

Charli likes for her Mom to pick her up
and walk around the house with her.

Charli posing for a photo.

Charli looks forward to traveling and adventure with her Forever Parents.

On road travel with her beautiful Yellow
Tulips for her Forever Mom.

Charli gets in position for her road trip.

Her adoptive parents set up the van for her comfort with a litter box, food and water.

Charli looks for outside friends and likes the adventure wherever she goes.

Charli likes to rest on the wind shield at a rest stop.

Resting at a night stop on her trip.

Charli enjoys the warmth of the fireplace.

Charli loves to cuddle when it's chilly out.

Charli is strapped in her seatbelt for her road trip.

Charli likes to cuddle with her Mom
while traveling in the van.

Charli has been to many places including
North Carolina, Tennessee, Key West,
and her second home in Georgia.

Charli in the window while on her
North Carolina adventure.

Charli is a hockey fan. She watches
hockey with her Mom.

They are both fans of the New York Rangers.

Charli loves to sleep on the furniture during the day.

Charli loves being in her own Home.

Harley and Bullseye the neighborhood cats
like to visit and show off for Charli.

Today, Charli is still very shy with some people,
but still curious to play with her outside friends.

Charli loves visiting and relaxing in
her Mom's Savannah home.

She props up on the books and is very comfortable.

Charli is very thankful for the love
from her forever parents.

Charli says goodbye for now.

The end.

In conclusion, please consider adopting an animal to give them the opportunity to love and be loved in their forever home. You will get unconditional love back.

For you see, inevitably every creature including Charli the cat needs to feel loved and secure.

Mr. Joey took that first step and adopted Charli, and with his love, her true personality developed. Mr. Joey gave her a forever home.

I hope you have enjoyed this love story and reach out to adopt an animal to spread love and joy.

I 🩶 you Charli, you made me so very happy to have you in my life!

I giggle every time we play together!

Ms. Theresa

An effigy of Charli found in an antique store.

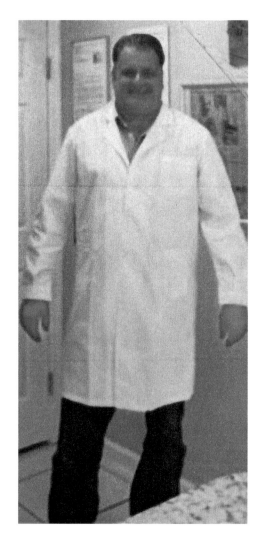

Forever Dad: Mr. Joey Passaro

From: New York

Dental Lab Technician/Owner

Hobbies: Motorcycles, Traveling, Adventure

Boat Captain: Southern Belle

About the Author:

Theresa Elizabeth (Ryan) Schopler

Registered Nurse

Children's Hospital, Cincinnati, Ohio

Presently works at: Atlantic Florida Dental, Inc.

Dental Implant Surgical Coordinator.

Hobbies: Playing piano, biking, swimming, boating, crafting, traveling, dancing

Note: The moral of the story is:

The posting that caught Mr. Joey's attention said the cat couldn't get along with other cats. Mr. Joey took the step to adopt Charli.He saved her from being placed in an animal shelter where she may have been passed over or worse

Mr. Joey's constant attention and patience with shy Charli turned into a loving relationship helping her to develop her true personality.

Ms. Theresa came into Charli's life with lots of love, giving Charli the security of a loving Forever Mom.

With the love of a Forever Dad and Forever Mom Charli came out of her shell and became fascinated with the outdoor animals and loved to play with her friends.

The posting that said Charli couldn't get along with other cats became an untruth.

Give an animal a chance for adoption and let them bring joy with love into your life.

Just look at her story of love and friendship.

This concludes the Beautiful Love 🩶 Story of Charli the Cat.

To be continued.

A major portion of the proceeds from the sale of the book will be donated to Broward County animal care and adoption.

In addition books will be sent to:

Nicklaus Children's Hospital
Cincinnati Children's Hospital
Joe DiMaggio Children's Hospital
Danny Thomas Children's Hospital